# Harry Potter Cookbook

Simple, Nutritious and Delicious Harry Potter Inspired Recipes in One Cookbook

By: Haylee Hall

Copyright 2020 Elaina Lewis

# License Notes

All rights reserved. No parts of this book shall be distributed, copied, shared, downloaded, posted, sold or otherwise reproduced without the written consent of the Author.

All instructions, suggestions, opinions and directions expressed in the content of this e-book are strictly for informational purposes. While the Author has made every attempt at accuracy, the Author accepts no liability for damages caused by following said content. The reader assumes all personal or commercial risk when following instructions, suggestions, opinions or directions in the content.

# Table of Contents

Introduction ..................................................................................6

   Madam Pomfrey's Pumpkin Juice Smoothie ................................8

   Mrs. Weasley's Corned Beef Sandwich .................................... 10

   Pumpkin Pasties ...................................................................... 13

   Pumpkin Pies + "Dobby's" Pies ................................................ 18

   Hagrid's Rock Cakes ................................................................ 22

   Polyjuice Potion Jelly Shots ..................................................... 25

   Harry Potter Butterbeer Pancakes............................................. 28

   Peanut Butter Sauce ................................................................ 32

   Warm and Hearty Mulligatawny Soup ...................................... 34

   Chocolate Ice Cream Cones..................................................... 37

   Knickerbocker Glory ................................................................ 40

Tender Roast Pork Loin .................................................................................. 44

Lemon Meringue Pie ...................................................................................... 46

English Fried Eggs and a Gammon of Bacon ............................................. 50

Poached Salmon in Honey and Dill Sauce ................................................. 52

Quidditch Players Pie .................................................................................... 54

Beef Lamb and Guinness Stew ..................................................................... 57

Butterbeer ........................................................................................................ 61

Butterbeer Cupcakes ..................................................................................... 63

Harry Potter Cauldron Cakes ....................................................................... 66

Weasley is Our King Cupcakes .................................................................... 69

Fruitcake with Nuts ....................................................................................... 72

Holiday Fruitcake ........................................................................................... 75

Harry Potter Treacle Tart .............................................................................. 79

Chocolate Frogs .............................................................................................. 82

Harry Potter Pumpkin Howlers .................................................................. 85

Coconut Crème Chocolate ......................................................................... 88

Steak and kidney pie ................................................................................. 90

Cornish pasties .......................................................................................... 93

Hat Pita Bread ........................................................................................... 96

Pumpkin Butterbeer Hot Chocolate ........................................................... 99

Raspberry Ice Cream ............................................................................... 102

Mini Peanut Butter Sandwich Cookies .................................................... 104

Eggnog Creams ........................................................................................ 107

Witches' Brew ......................................................................................... 109

Conclusion .................................................................................................... 111

Author's Afterthoughts ................................................................................. 112

About the Author .......................................................................................... 113

# Introduction

Eating is one of the principal abilities a child acquires alongside other psychomotor skills. Specialists affirm that eating well-nourished foods is one noteworthy approach to help diminish any danger of coronary illness and other unnatural conditions. What's more? It has been demonstrated that eating great sustenance adds to all-round development in people and creatures alike.

To have an adjusted eating routine, you should pick an assortment of nourishment on the grounds that no single food has all the supplements that the human body needs to develop rapidly. Your nourishment requires a total formation of all the essential supplements include vitamins A, B, C, D, E, and K. These vitamins are in egg yolk, natural products, vegetables, hamburgers, and fish. It drains and dairy items like cheddar, yogurt, spread, and cream, nuts, pork, yeast, grain, vegetables, chocolate, oil (vegetable and olive oils), margarine (produced using safflower, corn, and sunflower oil), et cetera. We know you need delectability, effortlessness, and nutritiousness all together. That is the reason we have for you in this book astounding formulas that you would love and appreciate. Swim in your fantasy when you taste the recipes. We got you covered.

# Madam Pomfrey's Pumpkin Juice Smoothie

This is not just any smoothie; it is one of the bests. Tastes great as you've never experienced! Why don't you try this yourself? 'To taste is to believe!'

**Serves** 4

**Cooks For** 15 minutes

**Ingredients**

- Two (2) chopped carrots
- Two (2) cored and peeled large apples
- Two (2) peeled bananas,
- Two (2) peeled oranges, and diced into small pieces (1 1/2)
- One (1) cup of pumpkin blend
- One (1) cup thick white coconut milk
- Two (2) cups of water
- One (1) teaspoon apple cider vinegar
- Two (2) teaspoons of cinnamon
- Half (1/2) teaspoon of ground ginger
- Half (1/2) teaspoon of ground cloves
- One (1) teaspoon of vanilla juice

**Directions**

Blend all Ingredients in a sizeable blender for about three to five minutes. Cool in the fridge and serve.

# Mrs. Weasley's Corned Beef Sandwich

Seriously speaking, this is one of the easiest recipes you would come across. This is Lunch-on-the-go for the world's busiest people.

**Serves** 4

**Cooks For** 40 to 45 minutes

**Ingredients**

- One (1) loaf unsliced Rye bread
- Two (2) pounds sliced corned beef, (check for DIRECTIONS)
- Twelve (12) ounces Russian dressing
- Twelve (12) ounces sauerkraut
- Twelve (12) of slices Swiss cheese
- Four (4) of tablespoons melted butter

**For Russian dressing:**

- 3/4 cup mayonnaise
- ¼ cup chili sauce
- Two (2) tablespoons of bittersweet cream
- Two (2) teaspoons of chopped flat-leaf parsley
- One and half (1 ½) tablespoons minced onion
- One and half (1 ½) tablespoons minced dill pickle
- Half (1/2) teaspoon fresh lemon juice
- Half (1/2) teaspoon of mustard powder
- Half (1/2) teaspoon of ketchup

## Directions

1. Before you begin, heat up the oven to 350°F.

2. Sprinkle the corned beef with some water and steam wrapped firmly in aluminum foil for some minutes in the oven.

3. Done that? Unwrap the rye bread and bake in the oven for about fifteen minutes, until you notice that the crust looks very crunchy. Remove bread from oven and set aside to cool for maybe five minutes.

4. When the rye bread is completely cool, slice into twelve pieces on a clean cutting board.

5. After that, take the corned beef out of the oven, unwrap it and expand each slice of bread with Russian dressing one after the other. Spread corned beef, sauerkraut, and slices of Swiss cheese covering half of the slices, and then top the sandwiches with the other slices.

6. Heat up two enormous heavy-sized skillets over medium heat. Spread butter on the bread. Let the sandwiches brown for about 7 minutes until you are satisfied. Then, turn the sandwiches upside down. Do the same with the other slices; make sure the cheese melts while doing this. Afterwards, cut each sandwich in half. And serve warm.

# Pumpkin Pasties

Making pumpkin pasties is easy. All you have to do is to follow the instructions keenly and, you are good to go. Make them and enjoy the feeling you must have had in the first episode of Harry Potter when you were introduced to this wonderful delicacy!

**Serves** 6

**Cooks For** 45 to 50 minutes + cooling time

**Ingredients**

**For the Pate Brisee**

- Two and half (2 ½) cups of all-purpose flour
- One (1) teaspoon of salt
- Two (2) tablespoons of table white sugar
- One (1) cup frozen unsalted butter
- Half (1/2) cup of ice water

**For the Pumpkin Pie filling**

- Six (6) jumbo eggs
- Four (4) cups of pumpkin blend
- One (1) cup of icing
- One (1) cup of brown sugar
- Three (3) teaspoons of ground cinnamon
- Two (2) teaspoons ground ginger
- One (1) teaspoon ground cloves
- One quarter (1 ¼) teaspoons ground nutmeg
- One quarter (1 ¼) teaspoons ground allspice
- Half (1/2) teaspoon ground mace spice

- One (1) teaspoon salt

**For Baking**

- Two (2) jumbo eggs (yolk separated from albumen)
- Two (2) tablespoons heavy Icing

**Directions**

**For Pate Brisee**

1. Prepare a medium-sized bowl. Pour the sugar, flour, margarine and salt, mix for some time. Add 1/4 container of the chill water gradually and mix again until you notice that the mixture clogs together and are the same size as crumbs.
2. Mould the batter into a levelled slab, wrap with plastic wrap and leave in the fridge for around sixty minutes.

**For Pumpkin Pie Filling**

1. Heat up the oven to 400°F.
2. Break eggs in a medium-sized bowl and whisk. Add in whipping cream, pumpkin blend and brown sugar, and mix to combine. Add the flavours and salt and mix well so they are combined. Prepare an oven dish and fill with the mixture, dig a pick into it, and bake for close to thirty to forty minutes until the point when the toothpick comes out clean and moist.
3. Set aside to cool.

**For Baking**

1. Spread the mixture out on a workspace until around the size of twelve inches.

2. Roll from the centre out and turn the crust quarter now and then so they don't stick to the surface of your workspace. Cut out as much as you can utilizing a small knife and move each to material paper-lined sheet. Place in the refrigerator for around thirty minutes or more.

3. Move batter out of the fridge when the pumpkin pie filling is totally cool and scoop a tablespoon of the filling into the centre of a mixture one after the other (this may take some time. But, it's all worth it in the end). Apply a thin layer of albumen around the edges using a pastry brush. Seal the edges and crease with a fork or your fingers to seal completely. Do the same with whatever is left of your mixture rounds. Place on the baking pan.

4. Combine the egg yolk together with the cream whisk carefully so it doesn't splash. Brush every one of the edges of the pasties. Dig about three to five openings in the top of every pasty using a small kitchen knife and place in the fridge for twenty-five minutes.

5. After that, heat up the stove to 400° F and cook until somewhat golden.

6. You can serve with any flavour of frozen yoghurt depending on your own preference.

# Pumpkin Pies + "Dobby's" Pies

A combination of two things in one is not ordinary! You might want to give it a try. You won't regret it.

**Serves** 3-4

**Cooks For** 10-20 minutes

**Ingredients**

**For Pumpkin Pies**

- One (1) can pumpkin blend, 8 ounces
- One (1) six ounces can of condensed milk,
- 1/4 cup of sugar
- Half (1/2) teaspoon of ground nutmeg
- Half (1/2) teaspoon of ground ginger
- 1/4 teaspoon of cinnamon
- 1/8 teaspoon ground cloves
- 1/4 teaspoon salt
- Two (2) jumbo eggs
- One (1) tablespoon of spice + One (1) tablespoon cinnamon
- Pie dough

**For Dobby's Pies**

- Three (3) medium-sized Irish potatoes, (peel and cut into small pieces)
- Half (1/2) diced medium sized onion
- One (1) grated carrot
- ¼ cup of frozen peas
- 1/3 cup of grated cheddar cheese
- Half (½) can of five ounces condensed mushroom soup cream
- Salt pepper
- Pie dough enough to make four-inch crusts

**Directions**

*Pumpkin Pies*

1. Heat the oven up to 425° F. Oil a medium-sized saucer and set aside.

2. Combine the sugar, salt, cloves, cinnamon, ginger and nutmeg and in a small mixer. Beat the two eggs, pumpkin and sugar-spice mixture in another mixer. Drain the condensed milk slowly to the pumpkin mixture and mix gently with a small spoon or spatula to combine. Drain the pumpkin mixture in a baking dish and bake for fifteen minutes.

3. Reduce the heat to 350° F, bake for twenty minutes more. Let cool on a flat wire tray.

4. Heat up the oven to 375° F again. Spread the pie crust until slightly thick. Divide the pastry into the circle of three-inch using a kitchen knife.

5. Scoop two tablespoons of pumpkin within the pastry circles one after the other, cover the circle and crease the edges.

6. Line baking pan with material paper and arrange all the pasties on it

7. Make small holes, about three or more as you want, at the top of each pastry, and brush lightly with the egg wash.

8. Sprinkle cinnamon sugar on the pasties and bake until they are light brown.

*Dobby's Pies*

1. Heat up the oven again to 400° F.

2. Combine the cheese, soup, onion, uncooked potatoes, peas, carrots, pepper, and salt in a large bowl, and stir.

3. Spread out the pastry, cut into three-inch circles, scoop one to two tablespoons of the vegetable mixture within the pastry, fold into two, and crease at the edges. Arrange pies on a parchment paper lined baking pan. Brush each pie with egg wash after making small holes in the top of each pastry

4. Turn oven onto 350° F and bake for ten minutes. Afterward, lower heat to 350° F and then bake for another thirty minutes more so they are light brown.

# Hagrid's Rock Cakes

This is not just "Hagrid Rock Cakes", it's something more. Until you have a taste of the marvelous combinations currants, raisins and sultanas you will not understand.

**Serves** 4

**Cooks For** 30-40 minutes

**Ingredients**

- Two (2) cups of all-purpose flour
- One (1) teaspoon of baking soda
- Half (1/2) teaspoon of salt
- Half (1/2) cup of frozen butter
- 1/3 cup of sugar
- One (1) teaspoon of vanilla juice
- 1/3 cup of currants + raisins + sultanas
- One (1) jumbo egg
- Two (2) tablespoons of milk
- Table sugar

**Directions**

1 Heat oven up to 400° F.

2 Line a large baking sheet using a parchment paper.

3 Combine the flour, baking soda and salt together in a large bowl and whisk, then add butter and turn lightly with your fingers until the mix is grainy. Add the sugar and currants and stir.

4 Beat the egg together with the milk and vanilla carefully. Add it into the flour mixture and turn until the pastry congests.

5 Shape dough into small balls, sprinkle with a generous amount of coarse sugar and arrange on a baking pan.

6 Bake for about fifteen minutes, until the tops of cakes are golden.

Remove from oven and set aside to cool. Serve.

# Polyjuice Potion Jelly Shots

Learn a new craft; lime, pineapple, and ginger ale! Potterers! Isn't this potterific?

**Serves** 4

**Cooks For** 45-50 minutes

## Ingredients

### For Ginger Ale mixture

- Half (1/2) cup of ginger ale
- One (1) plain gelatin
- Half (1/2) cup of ginger vodka

### For Pineapple mixture

- Half (1/2) cup of canned pineapple juice
- One (1) envelope plain gelatin
- Half (1/2) cup of pineapple vodka

### For Lime mixture

- Half (1/2) of cup water
- One (1) envelope plain gelatin
- Half (1/2) cup melted lime blend

## Directions

Prepare three gelatin mixes, as shown below:

**Pineapple**

Follow the instruction as for the ginger ale.

**Ginger Ale**

Add the ginger ale into a medium saucepan. Then sprinkle with the gelatin and soak for two minutes. Heat under low flame for about five minutes, stirring constantly, until the gelatin dissolves completely. Remove from heat and pour the vodka in.

**Lime**

Follow the instruction as for the ginger ale. Remove from heat and stir in the melted puree.

1. Drain mixtures into another bowl and place in the fridge until it is somewhat solid.
2. Prepare a standard medium-sized glass loaf pan. Spray with a little cooking spray (or pour in a drop of vegetable oil) and clean with a towel.
3. Stir each mixture quickly. Drop alternating spoonfuls of the three mixtures into the pan. Do this until the gelatin has been completely transferred. Place in the fridge for at least five hours so the gelatins can bond.
4. Cut into squares and serve.

# Harry Potter Butterbeer Pancakes

Surprise your friends and family with these delicious pancakes. It's never been better!

**Serves** 4

**Cooks For** 30 minutes

**Ingredients**

**For Pancakes**

- One (1) cup butterscotch chips
- Two quarter (2 ¼) cup of all-purpose flour
- Four (4) tablespoons of table sugar
- One (1) teaspoon of baking powder
- Half (½) teaspoon of baking soda
- Half (½) teaspoon of salt
- 3/4 cup of full milk
- Half (½) cup of cottage cheese
- Half (1/2) cup of coffee creamer
- 2 jumbo eggs

**For syrup**

- 1/4 cup of butter
- 1/3 cup of buttermilk
- Half (1/2) cup of sugar
- Half (1/2) teaspoon baking soda
- One (1) teaspoon of vanilla extract

**For Topping**

- One (1) cup heavy cream
- 1/4 cup powdered sugar
- Two (2) tablespoons instant dry butterscotch pudding mix
- Butterscotch Syrup (Optional)

**Directions**

**(Pancakes)**

1. Grind butterscotch chips into fine bits.
2. Combine flour, sugar, baking powder, baking soda, salt and butterscotch chip crumbs in a large bowl. Pour milk, ricotta, coffee creamer, and eggs in a separate bowl, and whisk together. Combine the Ingredients and stir well. Do not over-mix the batter so it does not become overly smooth.
3. Prepare a large cooking pan, spray with cooking spray and heat up over medium heat. Drain mix in using a half cup measuring cup. Let it cook for about two minutes until edges start to simmer, flip and do the same for the other side until it is golden brown.

**Syrup**

1. Done that? Pour butter, buttermilk, and sugar into a medium saucepan. Stir together on medium heat butter melts. Boil ingredients for about two minutes and remove from heat.
2. Stir in baking soda and butter extract. Leave for some minutes and it is ready to serve.
3. Pour all ingredients in a medium bowl and whisk until light and fluffy.
4. Top the pancakes with butter syrup and butterscotch icing.

# Peanut Butter Sauce

This rich and nutty peanut butter sauce is perfect for your salads. And it is also easy to make, in a few minutes everything is ready and "good to go". Enjoy.

**Serves** 8

**Cooks For** 20-25 minutes

**Ingredients**

- Two (2) cups of condensed coconut milk
- Eight (8) tablespoons peanut butter
- Three/Four (3/4) tablespoons curry paste
- Four teaspoons of soy sauce

**Directions**

Combine the above and mix well. Include some lime squeeze and taste. Add some more soy sauce if you want it saltier. Microwave for fifteen minutes and serve.

# Warm and Hearty Mulligatawny Soup

You will very much enjoy this soup. Tender chicken, delicious broth, heavenly coconut and rice to taste. Enjoy.

**Serves** 4

**Cooks For**

**Ingredients**

- One quarter (1 ¼) tablespoons of vegetable oil
- Two (2) chicken thighs
- Half (1/2) finely chopped onion
- One (1) julienned, diced carrot
- One (1) Brunoise diced celery ribs
- Three (3) of cups water
- Half (1/2), washed, peeled, cored, and diced all purpose apple (Brunoise diced)
- Half (1/2) tablespoon of curry
- Half (1/2) tablespoon of salt
- 1/4 teaspoon of fresh ground black pepper
- One (1) cup of boiled long grain white rice
- Shredded sweetened coconut

**Directions**

Set out a wide pot and heat oil in it. Sear the chicken under the high flame until the point when the two sides are golden. Remove chicken from the pot and put aside.

Drain the fat. Pour in the onions, carrots, and celery, and cook for around three minutes until the point that onions are soft and dark-colored. Pour in the water, apple, curry, salt, and pepper.

Return the chicken back to the pot and simmer. Reduce the heat and let simmer for thirty-five minutes, until the point the chicken is soft. Expel the chicken from the pot. Peel off the skin and remove the bones, cut the chicken into little strips, and return into the pot again. Skim the fat off from the surface of the pot. Pour the rice in and mix. Sprinkle some coconut on top and serve.

# Chocolate Ice Cream Cones

I tell you! It sometimes feels good to be alone, watch some TV having this tasty chilled chocolate ice cream. A trip to la la land and back.

**Serves** 10

**Cooks For** 30-35 minutes

**Ingredients**

- Four (4) cups of full milk
- Four (4) cups of thick cream
- 1 1/8 cups of table sugar
- Four (4) tablespoons of cocoa powder
- Ten (10) egg yolks
- Twelve (12) ounces melted and frozen chocolate
- Two (2) teaspoons of pure vanilla juice
- Sugar Cones

**Directions**

1. Drain milk in a medium-sized saucepan. Add cream, sugar, and cocoa powder and cook, stirring now and then until it's boiled. Add the dissolved chocolate in the egg yolks and whisk. Pour some of the hot milk into the yolks and mix to temper. Empty the yolk mix into the pot containing whatever is left of the milk mixture and cook, mixing always, until fairly hot.
2. Pour the mixture in through a strainer. Include the vanilla concentrate and mix until completely combined. Cover with cellophane and leave to cool to room temperature. After that, place in the fridge to chill.
3. Follow the maker's guidelines to make frozen yogurt. Pour in a tightly covered compartment and set aside until very firm.
4. Scoop dessert into each cone one after the other and add your fixings. Let it mollify at room temperature for fifteen minutes before you serve.

# Knickerbocker Glory

"Knickerbocker glory is an ice cream sundae that's served in a tall and large conical glass to be eaten with a distinctive long spoon,"Wikipedia.

**Serves** 8

**Cooks For** 45 minutes

**Ingredients**

- Four (3) cups of custard
- Four (4) cups prepared gelatin dessert Jell-O
- Chopped toast peanuts
- Four (4) cups chopped fresh berries
- Two (2) pint of vanilla ice cream
- Chocolate syrup
- For Custard
- Half (1/2) cup of table sugar
- Five (5) tablespoons of corn-starch
- Half (1/2) teaspoon of salt
- Two (2) cups of full milk
- Five (5) large egg yolks
- Two (2) teaspoons vanilla juice

**Directions** (Custard)

1. Combine two tablespoons of the sugar with the cornstarch and salt in a large saucepan. Add the milk and cream and stir slowly for some minutes until the cornstarch dissolves completely. In a separate bowl, beat the egg yolks and two tablespoons of sugar.

2. Boil the milk mixture over medium heat until its thick. Reduce the flame completely. Pour half cup of the hot mixture into the yolks to temper. Pour the yolk mixture into the saucepan and stir for some time.

3. Increase the heat back to medium. Cook until the mixture is thick. Remove the pan from the heat, add the vanilla and stir to incorporate.

4. Sieve the custard into a medium-sized bowl to separate lumps. Cover the custard with plastic wrap and let cool.

**For Icing**

- Two (2) cups heavy cream
- Five (5) tablespoons of icing sugar
- Two (2) teaspoons of fresh vanilla juice

**Directions**

Combine the heavy cream, sugar, and vanilla in a bowl and mix until completely thick.

**Directions**

1. Set up the custard, icing, and Jell-O before you start, and also cleave and toast the nuts also.
2. Wash, peel and chop the berries into small sizes.
3. Partition one and half quart of the frozen yogurt into six set out glasses. Equitably separate one measure of milk into the glasses. Afterward, separate one measure of the Jell-O over the fruits, measure of the custard over the Jell-O layer once again with the rest of the dessert, fruit, Jell-O, and custard.
4. Top with toasted nuts, whipped cream, and some chocolate syrup. Serve.

# Tender Roast Pork Loin

Follow the recipes through and you have yourself a tender and juicy pork loin to share with friends and family.

**Serves** 8

**Cooks For** 40-50 minutes

## Ingredients

- One and half (1 ½) teaspoons of salt
- Half (1/2) teaspoon of fresh ground black pepper
- Half (1/2) teaspoon of ground thyme
- Half (1/2) teaspoon of cinnamon
- Hot pepper
- Three (3) pounds pork loin

## Directions

1. Heat up the oven to 325°F.
2. Combine all ingredients, excluding the pork in a small bowl. Dip pork in the mixture and place on a roasting pan.
3. Roast for about thirty minutes. Remove the roast from the oven and let it cool. Carve and serve after fifteen minutes.

# Lemon Meringue Pie

This amazing delicacy dates back to the 19th century. So, the next time you want to make a dessert, let it be lemon meringue pie.

**Serves** 2

**Cooks For** 25-30 minutes

**Ingredients**

**For Crust Covering**

- One (1) container of universal handy flour
- One (1) tablespoon of table sugar
- ¼ teaspoon of salt
- ¼ stick (4 tablespoons) diced frozen margarine
- Two (2) tablespoons diced frozen vegetable shortening
- Two/three (2/3) tablespoons of chilled water

**For Filling**

- One (1) container of table sugar
- 1/4 container of corn-starch
- One (1) container of water
- Two (2) jumbo egg yolks, whisked
- 1/4 container of lemon juice
- Half (1/2) tablespoon of ground lemon peel
- 1/8 stick (2 tablespoons) margarine

**For Topping**

- Two (2) Jumbo egg whites
- 1/8 teaspoon of tartar cream
- 1/8 teaspoon of salt
- 1/4 teaspoon of unadulterated vanilla juice
- Half (1/2) cup table sugar

**Directions** (For the covering)

1. To make the pie covering, combine the flour, sugar, and salt in a bowl. Mix well to incorporate. Sprinkle and shortening over the mixture and mix until the point that the mixture is quite rough. Add margarine and mix again. Drain the mix out into a huge mixing dish. Include two to four tablespoons chill water over the mixture, turn using a spatula until the point that you notice the mixture is clumpy. Make the mixture together into a ball, pat it onto a plate and cover with a plastic wrap. Store in the fridge for some minutes.

2. Spread out the mixture into an eleven-inch circle on a floured surface. Fold pastry into half. Drain the mixture into the skillet; try to fit it in well so it doesn't enlarge. Leave one-inch of shade and trim the dough; join the shade under and crease the edges utilizing the teeth of your fork or your bare fingers. Place the outer layer in the fridge for around twenty minutes. Then, preheat the oven to 425°F.

3. Spread a sheet of aluminum foil inside the solid pie crust. Fill the outside layer with beans; let it heat for around twenty minutes until you notice that the crust is entirely dry. Decrease the temperature to 350°F, remove the thwart, and heat for around five minutes more, until the point that the outside is somewhat golden. Remove from the oven and put aside.

**For the filling**

1. Combine the sugar, corn-starch, and water in a medium-sized pan and mix until the corn-starch breaks up. Cook under low fire, mixing always, until the point when the mixture is thick. Include the yolks, whisk and cook, mixing often, until the point when the mixture is thick and gurgling. Set down from heat and add the lemon juice, lemon pizzazz, and margarine. Mix delicately until the point when everything totally breaks down.

2. For the meringue, whisk the egg whites, cream of tartar, salt, and vanilla in a different bowl. Add sugar to taste. Increase speed to medium-high and whisk egg whites until the point that they are firm (also ensure that they don't dry up).

Heat the oven up to 350°F. Drain the filling into the outer layer. Spread the meringue over the filling. Seal the edges tightly. Make twirls in the meringue with the spoon handle.

5. Bake the pie for around thirty minutes. Cool, and serve.

# English Fried Eggs and a Gammon of Bacon

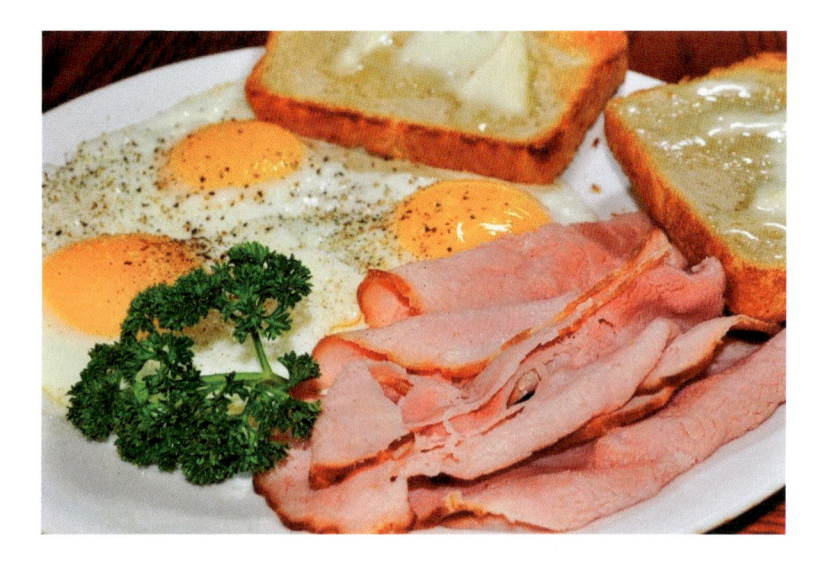

Have something "uniting" for breakfast. Let your buddy body know how much you care.

**Serves** 2

**Cooks For** 15 minutes

**Ingredients**

- Two (2) bacon gammon
- Two (2) tablespoons lard
- Four (4) jumbo eggs
- Salt + ground black pepper

**Directions**

- Heat a frying pan over medium-high heat. Sear the bacon in the skillet. After that, cook for four minutes. Flip the bacon using a flat spoon, and cook for about four minutes more, until you notice bacon is done and fresh.
- Remove the bacon. Empty fat out of the skillet.
- Lower the heat to medium-low. At the point when the remaining fat begins to sizzle, break eggs in a little bowl, pour in the container (don't whisk) and season with enough salt and pepper.

# Poached Salmon in Honey and Dill Sauce

Aside from the fact that this is Harry Potter related, it is also healthy and delicious. Enjoy.

**Serves** 2

**Cooks For** 45-50 minutes

**Ingredients**:

- One and half (1½) tablespoons of butter
- Half (½) burnoise chopped onion
- One (1) tablespoon all-purpose flour
- Half (1/2) cup of dry white wine
- Half (½) tablespoon of honey
- Half (½) tablespoon of burnoise chopped fresh dill
- One (1) pound fish fillet (Salmon preferably), rinsed, dried and cut into four pieces
- Salt + fresh ground black pepper

**Directions**

1. Melt the butter in a wide pot. Include the onions and cook for around five minutes, mixing always.
2. Add the flour, mix until bonded. Include the nectar as well as the wine. Cook, mixing always, until the mix is totally combined. Pour in the dill then.
3. Add a little shake of salt and pepper to the salmon filets. Let stew for twenty minutes after, tightly covered (the salmon separates when pricked about with a fork when set). Scrape the bottom of the pot for the stuck fillets while cooking and serve.

# Quidditch Players Pie

Before a game of Quidditch, this dish is usually served for dinner. Could it be maybe that it is a very filling, delicious and healthy meal? Or maybe it sharpens their vision? Well… I wouldn't know. Find out yourself!

**Serves** 2-4

**Cooks For** 45 minutes

**Ingredients**:

- Half (1/2) pound of ground beef
- One (1) medium ribbed and seeded green pepper
- Half (1/2) smashed and diced garlic clove
- 1/4 cup of chopped onion
- 1/4 cup of finely diced carrot
- 1/4 cup of frozen peas
- One (1) packet of Chicken Gravy mix (people usual use Beef meat gravy but you can use this for a doubled flavor taste)
- One (1) cup of mashed fresh potatoes
- Half (½) cup of shredded cheddar cheese

**Directions**

1. In a small saucepan, cook half of the Chicken gravy mix following the maker's directions and set aside
2. Cook the beef in a large saucepan for about six minutes. And when you notice it is brown, remove from heat. Then, drain fat and set aside.
3. Using the used skillet, reduce the flame to medium and add the onions, jalapenos, carrot, and garlic; cook until they are soft.
4. Add the peas, stir constantly, and warm for about three minutes. Add cooked gravy and beef; stir well to incorporate
5. Place ground beef mixture into a large lubricated skillet, spread the potatoes on the mixture, add cheese and sprinkle cheddar cheese. Place in the oven and bake for fifteen minutes on 350-degree in the oven, then, broil until cheese melts and is golden brown
6. Remove from oven. Cool and serve

# Beef Lamb and Guinness Stew

This is a classic you would want to give a try.

**Serves** 4-5

**Cooks For** 30-40 minutes

**Ingredients**

- Three (3) pounds of finely chopped beef
- Kitchen salt
- Fresh ground black pepper
- Four (4) tablespoons of unsalted butter
- Two (2) chopped large onions
- Four (4) minced garlic cloves
- Two (2) chopped carrots (Brunoise chopped)
- Two (2) ribs of Brunoise chopped celery
- Ten (10) shredded and sliced mushrooms
- Two (2) tablespoons of all-purpose flour
- Half (½) Spring will
- Two (2) cans of beer
- Eight (8) ounces grated cheddar
- Sherry vinegar
- Two (2) discs pie dough
- One (1) Jumbo egg

**Directions**

1. Heat the oven up to 375°F.
2. Add a liberal shake of salt and pepper to the beef and put aside.
3. Melt the butter under medium heat in earthenware and put aside.
4. Stir in the onions, garlic, and a touch of salt, and cook until delicate and brown. Mix in the carrots, celery, mushrooms, flour, and another touch of salt and cook until the point that they are relaxed and the mushroom shrinks. Pour the vegetables into a large mixing bowl and set aside. Roast the beef and transfer to the bowl of vegetables.
5. Pour in about a large portion of the lager into the earthenware, scraping consistently any bits with a flat spoon.
6. Turn the vegetables and hamburger once again into the earthenware and include the spring will and enough lager to cover the meat and vegetables. Place in the stove and let cook, covered, for seventy minutes.
7. Remove from the oven and stir. Return to the oven and cook for half an hour (make sure you cook uncovered until the liquid has reduced to a bit). Squeeze half of the cheddar in; add some of the seasonings, vinegar and salt for flavor.
8. Serve the stew and sprinkle with the left over cheddar

9. Roll out pie mixture rounds until 1/8-inch thick; isolate each round into quarters, and top ramekins with a bit of pie batter. Trim excess pastry, leaving an inch edge around, and tuck the remaining in, crease with a fork, make some holes in the middles.
10. Whisk the egg and a tablespoon of water together in a little mixing dish. Brush the pie mixture with the egg wash. Set the ramekins on a baking pan, and heat for around thirty minutes, or until the point that it's cooked up.
11. Serve warm

# Butterbeer

The best of beers you cannot have alone, but with several friends, laughing over old-school jokes.

**Serves** 2-4

**Cooks For** 15-20 minutes

**Ingredients**

- Two (2) tablespoons of caramel topping
- Two (2) bottles of creme soda
- For Whipped topping
- Half (1/2) cup of icing
- One (1) tablespoon of caramel topping
- 1/4 teaspoon of fresh vanilla juice
- One (1) tablespoon of table sugar

**Directions**

1. Pour one tablespoon of caramel garnish and 2 tablespoon cream soda each into four vast mugs. Stir until the point when caramel is separate and watery.
2. Drain the remaining soda into the mugs one after the other, so that each mug is almost full. Include icing, caramel, vanilla extract and sugar, and whip until the point that crests forms.
3. Serve.

# Butterbeer Cupcakes

These are not just "the cupcakes"; they are the brown, buttery, fluffy, vanilla-flavored butterbeer cupcakes, with butterscotch & sugar frosting.

**Serves** 5-8

**Cooks For** 40 minutes

**Ingredients**

**For Cupcakes**

- Half (1/2) box of yellow cake mix
- One (1) Jumbo egg
- 1/8 cup of vegetable oil
- 1/4 cup of vanilla creme soda
- 1/8 cup of granulated brown sugar
- Half (1/2) of 3.4 ounces pack of butterscotch pudding mix,

**For Icing:**

- 1/4 cup of butter
- Half (1/2) tablespoon of butterscotch sundae sauce
- 1/8 cup of brown sugar
- 1/8 teaspoon of butter extract
- Half (1/2) teaspoon of vanilla juice
- One (1) cup of icing sugar
- 1/8 cup of thick white milk (to be used when the frosting is too heavy)
- Butterscotch sauce

**Directions**

1. Heat stove up to 350°F. Set out two cake pans set with paper liners.

2. Mix the vanilla crème soda, eggs, oil, dry pudding mixture and some brown sugar and in a big bowl. Mix until totally combined. Fill in the mix equally in the biscuit containers until almost full.

3. Place the cupcakes in the grill and prepare for around fifteen minutes until a pick stuck inside turns out moist. Put aside to cool.

4. Combine the butter, butterscotch sauce, brown sugar, margarine and vanilla extracts in a bowl and mix well until smooth and soft. Include the icing sugar, one glass at any given moment, until the point when you see the icing is light (If the icing is too thick stream in some cream).

5. Siphon the icing onto the cupcakes, and sprinkle with some butterscotch sauce (If you want) and serve.

# Harry Potter Cauldron Cakes

These cupcakes are definitely worth it. Don't have this alone, share with your friends at a small get together!

**Serves** 2-4

**Cooks For** 20-30 minutes

**Ingredients**

**For Cakes:**

- One (1) box of yellow cake mix
- 3 jumbo eggs
- One (1) cup of bitter-sweet cream
- Half (½) cup of water
- ¼ cup of condensed milk
- Half (½) cup of groundnut oil
- Two (2) tablespoons of brown sugar
- One (1) teaspoon of vanilla

**For Filling:**

- Instant vanilla pudding
- food colouring

**Directions**

1. Heat stove up to 350°F.

2. Beat eggs, water, oil, dark-colored sugar and vanilla together until mixed. Include acrid cream, milk and cake mix. Mix until totally smooth.

3. Ladle into bake cups and arrange in the stove and prepare for twenty minutes or until the point that a toothpick jabbed within the mixture comes out.

**For Filling**

1. Prepare pudding following instructions on the label and then mix in food dye.

2. Make out small holes on each of the cupcakes using a tiny knife and fill with the vanilla pudding.

# Weasley is Our King Cupcakes

Crown yourself with some cupcakes that you will enjoy so much. The Weasley is our King Cupcakes is made to taste. Enjoy

**Serves** 3-4

**Cooks For** 40-45 minutes

**Ingredients**

**For Cake**

- Half (1/2) box of Yellow cake mix
- Half (1/2) teaspoon of cinnamon
- Dash nutmeg
- Half (1/2) teaspoon of vanilla
- Half (1/2) teaspoon of lemon peel

**For Filling**

- Two (2) tablespoons of melted butter
- Three (3) tablespoons of brown sugar
- Half (1/2) teaspoon of cinnamon
- One (1) teaspoon of Nutmeg
- 1/4 teaspoon of vanilla

**Icing**

- One (1) stick softened butter
- Two (2) cups of table sugar
- Half (1/2) teaspoon of vanilla
- Half (1/2) teaspoon of cinnamon
- One (1) cup of thick milk creme

**Directions**

1. Heat oven up to 350°F. Make cake mixture following maker's guidelines. Add the cinnamon, nutmeg, vanilla, and lemon pizzazz, and whisk.

2. Prepare a clean earthenware, arrange in cupcake papers and measure batter in. Add in the sugar, cinnamon, nutmeg, and vanilla into the margarine and mix well. Add a teaspoon of the mixture on of the cupcake batter. Spin with a toothpick. Mix the margarine for a couple of minutes, until totally soft. Include the sugar, vanilla, and cinnamon and keep on mixing until the point when combined all around.

3. Ladle on to the top of cupcakes. Sprinkle red, yellow, and white sugar to finish everything. Top with fondant crowns. (To make the crowns, you will need fondant. Cut a zigzag around the edges, dust with some gloss and add silver confects. Move them around to make the crown. Seal the edges together and leave until they are firm and sit on the cupcakes)

# Fruitcake with Nuts

Make your fruitcake taste better with the "nutty feeling"!

**Serves** 9

**Cooks For** 50-60 minutes

**Ingredients**

- One (1) cup of all-purpose flour
- 1/4 cup of fresh ground almonds
- Half (1/2) teaspoon of fresh ground cinnamon
- 1/4 teaspoon of ground allspice
- 1/8 teaspoon of ground nutmeg
- 1/8 teaspoon of ground cloves
- 1/8 teaspoon of salt
- One (1) sticks of butter
- Half (1/2) cup brown sugar
- Half (1/2) grated orange peel
- Half (1/2) grated lemon peel
- Two (2) jumbo eggs
- 1/8 cup of orange marmalade
- ¼ cup of dark raisins
- ¼ cup of golden raisins
- ¼ cup of sweetened dried cranberries
- 1/8 cup of fresh apple juice

**Directions**

1. Heat the oven up to 300°F. Then, add some vegetable oil and flour in a tall, big rectangular baking pan that is about two to three-inches deep and cover the bottom with parchment paper. Combine the flour, ground almonds, spices, and salt in a large mixing bowl and whisk.

2. In another large bowl, mix cream the butter, sugar, and zest of orange and lemon for about five minutes with an electric mixer, until the point that it's fluffy. Add the eggs one at the time and beat until incorporated. Add the marmalade and flour mixture and then the dark raisins, currants, and cranberries and stir in. Add the apple juice and stir. Stir again using a spatula to make sure the batter is evenly mixed. Drain the batter into the pan and bake for two hours. Afterward, remove from the oven and leave it to cool. Turn the cake out onto a sheet of aluminum foil and then remove the parchment paper. Serve with a nice cup of tea.

# Holiday Fruitcake

What makes this fruitcake different from the previous one? It is the combination of milk, blueberries, spice, fruits and all other things which makes it a yummy delight. And mind you, it's not only for the holidays. It can also serve your lunch.

**Serves** 10

**Cooks For** 50-60 minutes

**Ingredients**

- Half (1/2) cup of chopped ginger
- 2 cups of dried, chopped mango,
- One (1) cup of dried blueberries
- One and half (1 ½) cups of dried currants
- One and half (1 ½) cups of dried, chopped apricots
- One (1) cup of dried cranberries
- One (1) cup of dried cherries
- Lemon rind
- Orange rind
- One and half (1 ½) cups of rum
- One (1) cup of table sugar
- One (1) cup of brown sugar
- Two (2) stick of unsalted butter
- One (1) cup of fresh apple juice
- Four (4) tablespoons of condensed milk
- Two (2) teaspoons of ground cinnamon
- Half (1/2) teaspoon of ground allspice
- Half (1/2) teaspoon of ground garlic cloves
- Two (2) teaspoons of baking powder

- One (1) teaspoon of salt
- Two and half (2 ½) cups unbleached white flour
- Four (4) jumbo eggs
- One (1) cup of toasted and chopped pecans

**Directions**

1. Combine crystallized ginger, dried fruits, orange and lemon rinds, and rum in a large bowl, and soak for eight hours. (You can do this eight hours to the cooking to make things faster and easier)

2. Pour the mixture in a heavy saucepan; add the sugars (both the granulated white sugar and brown sugar), butter, apple juice, milk, and spices. Put stove on medium-high heat and boil the mixture, stirring constantly. Reduce the heat and let simmer for some minutes (eight minutes is ok). Remove from heat and set aside to cool.

3. Heat oven up to 325ºF. Sieve the dry ingredients into a bowl, transfer into the fruit mixture and stir well. Beat the eggs in a small bowl. Add to fruit mixture, stir well and fold in browned pecans.

4. Line a ten-inch coated bread pan with parchment paper. Drain mixture into the pan, poke a toothpick within and bake until a toothpick comes out clean and moist. When you remove from oven, allow the cake to cool, expel from pan, and serve.

# Harry Potter Treacle Tart

This is a traditional English dessert which can be served hot, warm or cold. It is even one of Harry Potter's personal bests.

**Serves** 4

**Cooks For** 30 minutes

**Ingredients**

**For Crust**

- Two (2) cups of 9 ounces all-purpose flour
- One (1) Stick + 1 tablespoon of four and half (4 ½) ounces
- unsalted butter
- Three (3) tablespoons of cold water

**For Filling**

- 1 3/4 cups of 14 ounces golden syrup
- Five and half (5 ½) ounces breadcrumbs
- Two (2) lemon juice and rind
- One (1) Jumbo egg (for the egg wash)

**Directions**

1. Pour the flour in a medium-sized mixing bowl. Mix in the butter until it is somewhat coarse. Add some water, mix well to incorporate. Press together to form pastry. Cover with plastic wrap and put in the fridge for thirty minutes.
2. Heat your oven up to 400°F. Oil a four quart sauté pan lightly and set aside.
3. Place five and half, two ounces of the pastry in the refrigerator to cool. Roll the remaining of the dough out into a ten-inch circle. Transfer into the pan and expand to the edges. Make tiny holes (two to three) in the pastry so as to prevent it from wheezing. Neatly trim its edges utilizing a kitchen knife so that there is only half inch left to extend. Set aside in the fridge.
4. Roll out the remaining pastry on a parchment paper. Brush with the egg wash and then set aside in the fridge.
5. Pour the golden syrup in a saucepan. Heat under low heat for one to 2 minutes. Add the lemon juice, the breadcrumbs, and zest, and then stir. Spread the mixture evenly into another ready pan.
6. Cut out half inch strips of the remaining dough that has been rolled out. Weave a lattice on the top. Bake for about until golden brown and serve (preferably, hot, warm or cold).

# Chocolate Frogs

It's even easier than you had thought. A fun flavor for your Harry Potter inspired parties.

**Serves** 6

**Cooks For** 15 – 20 minutes

**Ingredients**

- Two (2) pounds of hot milk chocolate
- For Peanut Butter Filling:
- One (1) cup of fresh peanut butter
- Half (1/2) cup + Four (4) tablespoons of icing sugar
- 1/4 teaspoon of salt
- Prepare a thermometer to temper the chocolate

**Directions**

1. Pour pure milk chocolate out into a bowl, and heat in the microwave on half power. Remove it after thirty seconds to stir. Warm for another twenty-five seconds. Repeat until chocolate is melted completely.
2. Carefully drain the melted chocolate into the frog molds and place in the fridge to freeze. Utilize a good silicone basting brush to coat inside the form. Make sure that the molds filled up.
3. For Peanut Butter Filling:
4. Meanwhile, combine the icing sugar, salt, and peanut butter in a bowl and stir together until well combined. Measure one tablespoon of the peanut butter mixture using small ice cream scoops. Place the scoops on a plate and place in the fridge to cool.
5. When the chocolate is ready. Divide the balls in half, spread out and fit into the mold, making sure there is still enough room atop the chocolate layer. Return in the fridge to chill. Repeat the process for the remaining melted chocolate.
6. When the chocolate is done, expel all the chocolate frogs from the molds. Cool and serve.

# Harry Potter Pumpkin Howlers

In Harry Potter, we all know receiving howlers means you have done something very inappropriate. You can reignite your imagination by making this different type of howlers made up from eggroll wrappers, cheese, and oil. Enjoy.

**Serves** 4-6

**Cooks For** 30 minutes

**Ingredients:**

- Twelve (12) eggroll wrappers
- Three (3) eggroll wrappers cut into four equal parts
- One (1) egg + One (1) teaspoon of water for egg wash
- Vegetable oil
- Black icing
- Red icing

**For filling**

- Eight (8) ounces of cheese
- Two (2) tablespoons of pumpkin blend
- One (1) tablespoon of brown sugar
- ¼ teaspoon of cinnamon
- Half (½) teaspoon of nutmeg
- Half (½) teaspoon of salt

**Directions**

1. Pour the cinnamon, cheese, brown sugar, pumpkin, nutmeg and salt in a sizeable bowl and stir to combine. Add a tablespoon of filling in the centre.
2. Dab eggwash around the edges and place over the filling. Afterwards, press together to seal. Dab with more egg wash and form into a shape of an envelope
3. Heat oil in a heavy skillet to 350°F. Fry the envelopes for three minutes on each side until golden brown.
4. When cool, decorate with eyes and lips with black and red icing respectively and serve.

# Coconut Crème Chocolate

For coconut lovers, this is especially for you!

**Serves** 4-6 dozen

**Cooks For** 15 min. + chilling

**Ingredients**

- Two (2) jars of 7 ounces, cholesterol free marshmallow crème
- Four (4) cups of sweetened, toast frayed coconut
- Two (2) teaspoons of vanilla juice
- Salt
- Two (2), Five (5) ounces each, chocolate milk candy bar
- Three (3) teaspoons shortening

**Directions**

1. Mix vanilla, marshmallow crème, coconut, and salt in a large bowl, until completely combined. Cover with cellophane and place in the fridge to cool.

2. Form mix into one and half inches' balls. Transfer into a parchment paper lined baking pan. Cover and place in the fridge to cool.

3. Combine chocolate and shortening and temper in the microwave, stir until completely smooth. Spread out a parchment paper; dip coconut balls in chocolate transfer on it. Leave to set and serve

# Steak and kidney pie

This pie is a true demonstration of the fine British cooking with its combination of braising steak, beef and lamb kidney. Cook slowly under medium heat to tender the beef well.

**Serves** 2

**Cooks For** 1 to 2 hours

**Ingredients**

- 6 ounces of puff pastry
- One (1) egg + One (1) extra egg yolk, mixed

**For the filling**

- One (1) tablespoon vegetable oil
- Twelve (12) ounces of diced braising steak
- Four (4) ounces of diced lamb kidney
- One (1) medium onion
- One (1) cup of plain flour
- One-pint of beef stock
- Salt + fresh ground black pepper
- A dash of ketchup

**Directions**

1. Heat up stove to 425°F
2. Boil the vegetable oil in a huge sauté pot; brown the hamburger (in clumps) all over. Brown the kidneys also in the same pot. Add some onions and cook for four minutes. Return the hamburger and sprinkle flour over the meat and onions to coat. Add the meat stock, mix well and boil.
3. Reduce heat and let stew with the pot open for forty-five minutes. Remove from heat. Include salt, pepper and ketchup and put aside to cool. Transfer the cooked meat mixture into a small dish. Set out the pastry thick.
4. Place the pastry on top of the pie dish. Trim the edges with your fingers. Brush the surface with the beaten egg mixture and prepare for thirty to forty minutes until slightly brown. Serve with steamed vegetables.

# Cornish pasties

It'll be wrong not to tell you that this pasty, which originated from Cornwall, United Kingdom, is filling, delicious and healthy. This is a great treat! I bet that's what you'll have to say after you taste this. It's definitely worth the time.

**Serves** 4

**Cooks For** 1 1/2 hour

**Ingredients**

**For the pastry**

- Fourteen (14) ounces of bread flour
- Two (2) ounces of suet
- Half (1/2) teaspoon of salt
- 1 ounce of butter
- One and half (1 ½) large cups of cold water
- One (1) egg, whisked with 1/8 teaspoon of salt

**For the filling**

- Six (6) ounces of braising steak
- Six (6) ounces of waxy potatoes
- Three and half (3.5) ounces of Swede
- Six (6) ounces of onions
- Salt + fresh ground black pepper
- One (1) stick of butter

**Directions**

1. Pour flour in a bowl; add the shortening, salt, butter and a lot of the water. Mix gently using a spatula. Transfer the ingredients into a non-sticking dough that is dry. Turn out the dough onto a clean workspace.

2. Mold the dough to combine the ingredients. Spread and make back into a ball, stretch and move it up once more. Repeat this again and again for five to six minutes. Make sure the mixture is smooth and shiny. Cover and put aside in the fridge for thirty minutes to one hour.

3. Meanwhile, peel and cut the potato, Swede, and onion into 1/4 inches cubes. Cut meat into fair sizes. Pour in a bowl and mix well. Include salt and ground dark pepper to season. Set aside for some time to set.

4. Oil a baking pan and line with a no-silicon-proof heating paper. Heat up the stove to 350°F. Take the dough out of the fridge and gap into four equal pieces. Roll each into a ball and spread. Spoon filling into each circle, spread the filling on half of the circle and leave the other half free. Drop a little margarine atop of the filling. Fold over the pastry, join and seal edges with your fingers. Then, fold under. Place pastries onto the heating plate, brush the top with the egg and salt mixture and prepare for around forty-five to fifty minutes in the stove until the point that the pastries are brown. Serve.

# Hat Pita Bread

Having a bad day, this is perfect for you. The taste of this refreshing bread will revive you. Come alive!

**Serves** 2-4

**Cooks For** 1-2 hours

**Ingredients**

- Half (1/2) teaspoon of dry yeast
- Half (1/2) teaspoon of sugar
- 1 1/4 cups of warm water
- One (1) cup of whole wheat flour
- Half (1/2) tablespoon of salt
- Half (1/2) tablespoon of olive oil
- Two (2) cups of flour

**Directions**

**For bread dough**

1. Pour warm water in a huge bowl and add sugar. Pour in the yeast and mix well.

2. Pour the entire wheat flour, one glass after the other, once the yeast is bubbly and mix again until the point when the mixture is smooth. Set aside for thirty minutes

3. Afterward, stir in the salt and olive oil, and then the flour. Mix in a stand mixer for around six to seven minutes. Transfer in bowl, cover with plastic wrap and set aside for two to three hours so that it expands.

4. Heat oven up to 350°F.

**For shaping and baking of bread**

1. Construct huge cone, around eight inches tall and six inches wide. Collapse dough tenderly and take two or three of it; put aside the remaining and cover.

2. Spread the mixture out in a huge circle, sufficient enough to cover the cone. Spray cone with non-stick shower and after that cover gently with your dough. Place the batter, upside down on a baking sheet.

3. Form a huge circle with the rest of the batter, around seven to eight-inches wide. Place it in a large material-lined coated baking pan. Ensure the focal point of the circle is level, and after that, wrinkle the edges to fit in the skillet. Bake until set. Remove from the oven and put aside.

4. Increase the heat of the oven to 425°F. Brush the bread with melted margarine. Stand the dough up straight. Replace the plate of bread back in the broiler and prepare for seventeen to twenty minutes until the point that you see bread is brown. Let cool a bit on a cooling rack. Serve.

# Pumpkin Butterbeer Hot Chocolate

This butterbeer hot chocolate is so delicious that when you taste it, it brings back all the interesting memories you had as a kid.

**Cooks For** 20-25 minutes

**Serves** 6

**Ingredients**

- Six (6) cups of full milk
- Half (1/2) cup of cocoa powder
- Two (2) teaspoons of ground cinnamon
- Twelve (12) ounces of chopped milk chocolate
- One (1) cup of pumpkin blend
- 1 1/3 cups of butterscotch
- Two (2) tablespoons of vanilla juice
- Four (4) tablespoons of butter
- Four (4) tablespoons of fresh bourbon

**For Butterscotch Cream**

- Two (2) cups heavy icing
- Four (4) tablespoons of butterscotch sauce
- One (1) teaspoon of vanilla juice

**Directions**

1. Pour milk to a large pot. Add the cocoa powder, butterscotch sauce, cinnamon, milk chocolate, vanilla, pumpkin, butter and whiskey. Boil, stirring regularly so that nothing burns.

2. Meanwhile, make the butterscotch icing. Whisk the cream in a large mixing bowl until stiff peaks form. Add in the vanilla mix well again. Add the butterscotch and stir, leaving streaks in the icing. Set aside in the fridge until ready to serve.

3. Spoon chocolate into mugs when hot and steaming, and dollop with cream.

**For Butterscotch Sauce**

1. Drop butter in a small saucepot and melt. Add the brown sugar, heavy icing and salt. Boil for four to five minutes on medium-low heat. Set down and stir in the vanilla and bourbon.

# Raspberry Ice Cream

With just seven simple **Ingredients**, you can have your ice cream cravings satisfied. Enjoy this healthy less-than-twenty-minutes raspberry ice cream with friends and family.

**Serves** 2

**Cooks For** 25 min.

## Ingredients

- Two (2) cups of half-and-half creme
- One (1) cup fresh of raspberries
- Half (1/2) cup of sugar
- Four (4) tablespoons of evaporated milk
- Two (2) teaspoons of vanilla juice
- Eight (8) cups of roughly crushed ice
- One and half (1 ½) cups of salt

## Directions

1 Prepare doubled quart-size re-sealable plastic bags. Fill the inner bag with the cream, milk, vanilla extract, raspberries and sugar and seal both bags, expelling just enough air.

2 Place the bags in a gallon-size re-sealable plastic freezer bag. Add ice and salt. Seal bag. Press bag to expel enough air. Wrap the bags in a kitchen towel and shake the cream mixture until it is thick.

# Mini Peanut Butter Sandwich Cookies

To ensure you get a smooth peanut butter, use your hand or an electric mixer to mix until preferably smooth, so you can enjoy together with friends.

**Cooks For** 45-55 minutes + cooling time

**Serves** 8

**Ingredients**

- Four (4) cups of shortening
- Two (2) cups of creamy peanut butter
- Two 2 cups of table sugar
- Two (2) cups of brown sugar
- Six (6) Jumbo Eggs
- Two (2) teaspoons of vanilla juice
- Six (6) cups of all-purpose flour
- Four (4) teaspoons of baking soda
- One (1) teaspoon of salt

**For Filling**

- One and half (1 ½) cups of creamy peanut butter
- One (1) cup of condensed milk
- Three (3) vanilla juice
- Six (6) cups of icing sugar

**Directions**

1. Heat up the oven to 350°F. Combine peanut butter, cream, shortening, and sugars in a large bowl and mix until blended. Beat in the vanilla and eggs. Whisk baking soda, flour, and salt gradually in another bowl until creamy.

2. Shape into one-inch balls. Arrange on baking pans. Bake for about eleven to thirteen minutes until done. Place on a cake rack to cool completely.

3. Mix vanilla, milk and peanut butter in a small bowl until combined. Add in icing sugar and mix well. Brush filling on the bottoms the cookies; place the remaining cookies on top.

# Eggnog Creams

'Crèmeanglaise' (English cream). That's what the Frenchs call it, for its rich and creamy taste. Make it your next dessert.

**Cooks For** 45 min. + Cooling time

**Serves** 2-3

**Ingredients**

- 3/2 cup flavoured white baking chips, divided
- ¼ cup of softened butter
- One ad half (1 ½) ounces of softened cream cheese
- One (1) tablespoon of dark rum
- 1/8 teaspoon of vanilla juice
- One (1) tablespoon of shortening
- Half (1/2) teaspoon of ground nutmeg

**Directions**

1. Dissolve half cup of the baking chips in a microwave and stirring now and then until it's smooth. Combine cream butter and cream cheese in a small bowl and mix until completely smooth. Add in the rum and vanilla. Afterward, mix in the melted chips. Cover and put in the fridge to set.
2. Shape mixture into one-inch balls and arrange on a paper-lined baking pan. Put in the refrigerator for Two hours until dry and firm.
3. Dissolve remaining baking chips and shortening in a microwave. Stir well until smooth. Dip balls in mixture. Replace on baking sheet and sprinkle with nutmeg. Place in the fridge to set.

# Witches' Brew

This is not a strange, scary concoction. It's something better; a tasty and colorful soup to be enjoyed. Enjoy.

**Cooks For** 20 min. + chilling

**Serves** 12

**Ingredients**

- One (1) cup of sugar
- Two (2) cups of water
- Ten (10) medium size kiwifruit, peeled and cut into fourths
- One (1) cup of fresh mint leaves
- Two (2) liters of chilled ginger ale
- One (1) cup of Ice cubes

**Directions**

1 Boil water and sugar in a tiny saucepan stirring constantly until sugar dissolves completely and set aside.

2 Blend the kiwi, mint and sugar syrup in a blender until it's completely mixed. Transfer into a large jug, stir in vodka and chill in the fridge. Add in some ginger ale then serve chilled.

# Conclusion

All has been said, now it is dependent upon you to complete the job. You need not disturb yourself any longer if you want to enjoy delicious foods that you must have come across in the course of reading through the amazing HarrryPotter. You don't need to think too much when you want to set up that 'all-squib' gathering for your astonishing little kids.

You have already found out that, with a line-up of easy recipes, you can acquire enough skills so you can consciously cook up delicious, as well as interesting meals in your kitchen, anytime.

We hope we have been able to satisfy you. Now you don't need to visit your long-time friends when you want to enjoy these meals. Everything has been conjured up, just for you and you alone.

# Author's Afterthoughts

You will not regret your choice to buy my book and read it from beginning to end! Thank you for taking precious time out of your day to peruse my work and try a recipe or two. My hope is that you find benefit within its pages and your culinary skills progress beyond the content.

There is an overwhelming variety of choices in the world today, so the fact that you considered your options and decided to take a chance on my work fills me with gratitude.

Fill in an online review on Amazon and let me know what you thought! Don't hold back, I want your honest opinion. Others will benefit from your experience and I will get the necessary feedback I need to create better books in the future!

*Thank you,*

*Haylee Hall*

# About the Author

Haylee Hall is a talented cookbook writer and chef living in Chesterland Ohio with her husband and four children. She graduated from the International Culinary Arts and Sciences Institute in Chesterland and went on to serve as head chef in some of Ohio's most prestigious restaurants.

Hall has won many local and national cooking awards and she excels in Mediterranean cuisine. When Haylee took a family trip to Malta as a teenager, she fell in love with the food. The smells and tastes of the local cuisine found a place in her heart and she never forgot how it made her feel. Hall went back to Malta and had the chance to take some courses at the Mediterranean Culinary Academy. She brought her newly learned techniques home to Ohio to share with her customers. Haylee has often said that she would like to retire somewhere in the Mediterranean and open up a small, intimate restaurant near the water.

With her success writing e-books and her culinary career flourishing, it is certain her dreams of retiring in a warm, tropical climate will become a reality. For now, her online cookbooks will spread the joy of cooking to readers all over the world. Keep an eye out for more cookbooks containing delicious recipes and helpful tips coming out soon.

Printed in Great Britain
by Amazon